THE GREAT BOOKS FOUNDATION
Discussion Guide
for Leaders

FROM THERE TO HERE

About Perfection Learning

Founded by two educators, Perfection Learning is a family-owned company that has provided innovative, effective reading, literature, and language arts materials to K–12 classroom teachers for more than seventy-five years. Developed over the course of three years, the *Literature & Thought* series is a breakthrough program designed to teach middle school and high school students to be critical readers and thinkers. Each *Literature & Thought* anthology is structured to help students explore an essential question by reading relevant, thought-provoking selections in a literary genre, literary theme, or historical era.

About the Great Books Foundation

The Great Books Foundation is an independent, nonprofit educational organization whose mission is to help people learn to think and share ideas. Toward this end, the Foundation publishes reading anthologies of challenging literature for all ages and offers workshops specifically designed to help teachers use the *shared inquiry* method in the classroom.

The Great Books Foundation was established in 1947 to promote liberal education for the general public. In 1962, the Foundation extended its mission to children with the introduction of Junior Great Books. Since its inception, the Foundation has helped thousands of people throughout the United States and in other countries begin their own discussion groups in schools, libraries, and community centers. Today, Foundation instructors conduct hundreds of workshops each year, in which educators and parents learn to lead shared inquiry discussion.

THE GREAT BOOKS FOUNDATION
Discussion Guide
for Leaders

FROM THERE TO HERE

Perfection Learning ∽ *LITERATURE & THOUGHT*

The Great Books Foundation
A nonprofit educational organization

Printed in the United States of America
4 5 6 7 8 9 PP 13 12 11 10 09 08
Published and distributed by

The Great Books Foundation
A nonprofit educational organization
35 East Wacker Drive, Suite 2300
Chicago, IL 60601-2298

www.greatbooks.org

CONTENTS

INTRODUCTION

This Discussion Guide for *From There to Here: The Immigrant Experience* focuses on several selections that the Great Books Foundation recommends for close reading and discussion using the Foundation's *shared inquiry* method. This collaborative, inquiry-based process complements the critical thinking encouraged by Perfection Learning's *Literature & Thought* series, and will inform your students' thinking about the essential question, "Should we keep America's immigration door open?" posed at the beginning of the book.

Shared inquiry is the effort to achieve a better understanding of a text by discussing questions, responses, and insights with others. For both the leader and the participants, careful listening is essential. The leader guides the discussion by asking questions about specific ideas and problems of meaning in the text, but does not seek to impose his or her own interpretation on the group. To be an effective leader of Shared Inquiry Discussion, training from the Great Books Foundation is strongly recommended.

The Great Books Foundation offers a range of professional development opportunities for discussion leaders, including an introductory two-day workshop and advanced workshops in the practice of shared inquiry. Participants learn how to frame questions that genuinely engage students, use follow-up questions to explore students' ideas more thoughtfully, and involve students of all abilities in focused, lively discussions. Instructors from the Foundation are also available for follow-up consultation days, which include classroom demonstrations and coaching. For more information, call the Foundation at 1-800-222-5870 or visit our Web site at www.greatbooks.org.

The shared inquiry approach develops students' reading comprehension in the context of thinking about genuine problems of meaning raised by a selection. The interpretive activities suggested in this Discussion Guide are designed to help students become more aware of their reactions as they read, develop a sensitivity to language, and value their own curiosity about a text. The focus on interpretation and discussion means that all students can participate confidently and improve their abilities to read and think critically about literature.

Your Role
as Leader

As the discussion leader, you serve as a model of an involved, curious thinker. By asking open-ended questions and showing genuine interest in your students' ideas, you help everyone reach a greater understanding of the selection.

We recommend that you prepare for each discussion unit by reading the selection closely and noting your own reactions and questions. Your preparation is as important as that of your students; knowing the selection well enables you to lead effectively. During your second reading, you may wish to mark the selection using the suggested note-taking prompt. These preparatory steps will help you consider the interpretive issues that the selection raises and plan your class schedule of activities.

SAMPLE SCHEDULES
OF ACTIVITIES

In-class work on a Great Books discussion unit consists of

- Reading the selection aloud and identifying questions worth exploring (Sharing Questions)

- Rereading the selection, taking notes (Directed Notes), and comparing those notes with others

- Shared Inquiry Discussion, the culminating activity in which interpretive questions are explored in depth

The activities that precede discussion—the Text Opener, reading the selection aloud, Sharing Questions, and a second reading with Directed Notes—will help students think for themselves about the selection and prepare them to develop their own interpretations in discussion. Most teachers will want to extend this process with the suggested Writing After Discussion activities, which encourage further reflection on the issues raised by the selection and give students the opportunity to synthesize and elaborate on their ideas, making them relevant to their own lives.

Following are two sample weekly schedules. The length of the in-class sessions will vary according to the length of the selection. Depending on your students' needs, you may choose to assign some activities as homework.

Option A: Three In-class Sessions

Session 1

- Text Opener *(optional)*
- First reading of the selection
- Sharing Questions

Session 2

- Second reading with Directed Notes
- Comparing and discussing notes

Session 3

- Shared Inquiry Discussion

Homework: Writing After Discussion *(optional)*

Option B: Two In-class Sessions

Session 1

- First reading of the selection
- Sharing Questions

Homework: Second reading with Directed Notes

Session 2

- Comparing and discussing notes
- Shared Inquiry Discussion

Homework: Writing After Discussion *(optional)*

Conducting the Interpretive Activities

Text Opener: 10–20 minutes *(optional)*

- Sparks students' interest in the selection by introducing a theme or issue they will encounter in the text

- Helps students connect their own experiences to the text

Before the first reading, you may choose to conduct the Text Opener with students, particularly if the selection is likely to prove challenging or foreign to them. A short discussion of students' responses is sufficient, since the goal is to spur their interest in reading the selection. You may wish to have students write briefly (for no more than five minutes) before discussing their responses.

First Reading: 10–15 minutes *(depends on selection length)*

- Allows students to enjoy the story

- Helps students take in unfamiliar vocabulary

- Gives students the model of a fluent reader using appropriate pace and expression

- Ensures that all students begin their interpretive work on an equal footing

- Leads naturally to students sharing questions about the selection

We recommend reading the selection aloud to your students as they follow along in their books and note questions that occur to them.

Sharing Questions: 15–20 minutes

- Teaches students that their curiosity and desire to know are starting points for interpretive thinking

- Develops the habit of reflecting and questioning after reading

- Clears up initial misreadings and comprehension difficulties

- Generates questions worth exploring in discussion

- Fosters a cooperative atmosphere in which students are comfortable raising questions to explore with the group

After the first reading, ask for students' initial reactions to the selection *(What did you think? How did you like it?),* then encourage them to ask any questions they have about the selection, including vocabulary questions (see p. 25). You should briefly consider possible answers to students' questions and clear up any issues that interfere with comprehension, while identifying other questions to be considered further in discussion. We recommend that you write down students' questions, perhaps posting them on the board or on chart paper for all to see. Looking over students' questions after the session is an excellent way to gauge their curiosity and to plan your discussion of the selection.

Second Reading with Directed Notes: 25–40 minutes

- Gives students guided practice in deciding which parts of a text require closer examination

- Improves students' ability to recall and use supporting evidence for their opinions

- Helps students draw connections as they read and recognize interpretive issues

- Helps students recognize that a passage can have different interpretations

- Encourages the habit of using notes as a way of reacting to and thinking about literature

Reading twice and taking notes during the second reading are distinctive features of Great Books programs and may be new to students. We recommend that you explain to students the reasons for rereading and note taking: this careful consideration of the text deepens understanding, and written notes offer readers a way to think about, remember, and share their reactions to a story.

Suggested note-taking prompts for each selection highlight interpretive issues in the text. Marking the text according to the prompt makes it easy to compare the reactions of different individuals to the same passage. The following suggestions will help your students get the most out of note taking:

- Allow time for students to discuss some of their notes, so that they see different interpretive possibilities and understand the value of explaining their notes to others.

- Lead a brief discussion of students' notes on one or two pages of the selection, asking students to share not only what they marked but also the thinking behind their notes.

- Ask questions like *Why did you mark the passage that way? Did anyone else mark it that way? Did anyone mark it differently? Why?* to help students understand both their thinking and that of others.

- You may also choose to have students discuss their notes in pairs while you circulate through the room, asking follow-up questions as needed.

Here are examples of how two different students marked the same poem when asked to mark the **negative** consequences of going through or not going through the door with **N,** and the **positive** consequences with **P.**

FROM THERE TO HERE
The Immigrant Experience

PROSPECTIVE IMMIGRANTS PLEASE NOTE

Either you will
go through this door
or you will not go through.

If you go through
there is always the risk
of remembering your name.

Things look at you doubly
and you must look back
and let them happen.

If you do not go through
it is possible
to live worthily

to maintain your attitudes
to hold your position
to die bravely

but much will blind you,
much will evade you,
at what cost who knows?

The door itself
makes no promises.
It is only a door.

ADRIENNE RICH

If you go
through
N/P — Why
is remembering
your name
a "risk"?

Positive to
not go
through — stay
who you are,
live worthily

Negative to
not go through—
lessons not
learned

From There to Here
The Immigrant Experience

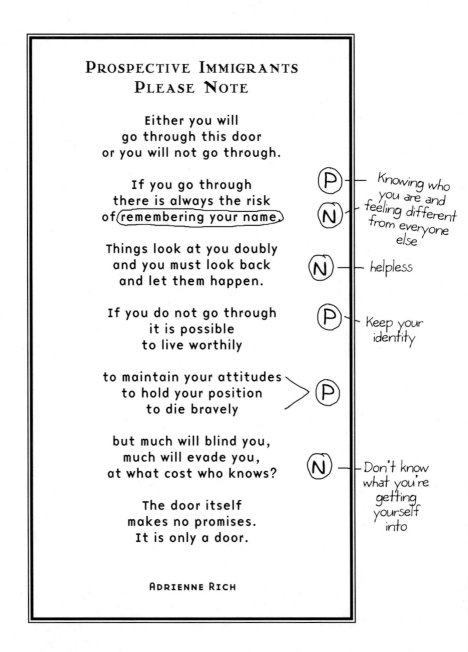

PROSPECTIVE IMMIGRANTS
PLEASE NOTE

Either you will
go through this door
or you will not go through.

If you go through
there is always the risk
of remembering your name.

Things look at you doubly
and you must look back
and let them happen.

If you do not go through
it is possible
to live worthily

to maintain your attitudes
to hold your position
to die bravely

but much will blind you,
much will evade you,
at what cost who knows?

The door itself
makes no promises.
It is only a door.

ADRIENNE RICH

(P)
(N) — Knowing who you are and feeling different from everyone else

(N) — helpless

(P) — Keep your identity

(P)

(N) — Don't know what you're getting yourself into

Shared Inquiry Discussion: 30–45 minutes

- Encourages students to present arguments clearly and persuasively, to offer reasons for their opinions and inferences, and to support their ideas with evidence

- Helps students analyze character motivation and development, as well as cause and effect

- Helps students learn to weigh the merits of opposing arguments and to modify their initial opinions

- Gives students the confidence to shape and express their own opinions about what they read

- Gives students practice in active listening and cooperative learning

In this cornerstone activity of Great Books programs, students work together to interpret the text, guided by the open-ended questioning of the leader. We recommend that students be given time to reflect individually on the leader's opening question before discussion begins, so that they can gather their thoughts and examine the text for evidence. Having students write down their answers on the Building Your Answer activity page (pp. 22–23) is an excellent way to begin discussion, and enables you to call on less vocal students knowing that they have something to contribute. The Building Your Answer page also includes a portion for use at the end of discussion, to encourage students to reconsider their initial answers.

While this guide provides discussion questions for each unit, we encourage you to use these in combination with questions generated by you or your students. Focus questions appear in boldface type, followed by a group of related questions; these can be used in any order depending on the progress of the discussion, the needs of your students, and your teaching goals.

Creating a Good Environment for
Shared Inquiry Discussion

Establishing an atmosphere that promotes discussion involves preparing both the classroom and the students themselves.

Setting up the classroom. Try to arrange the room so that everyone can see and hear each other. Your students should have a convenient surface on which to place their books and open them up. Ideally, have students sit around a table or arrange their desks in a circle or square. This type of arrangement stimulates discussion and helps students realize that the ideas offered by their classmates can be a major source of insight into a selection. If it isn't possible to arrange the room in this way, encourage students to look at the person talking, acknowledging one another and not just the leader.

Introducing students to shared inquiry. For some students, it will be a new idea that you will not be providing answers but instead asking open-ended questions with more than one reasonable answer. Emphasize to students that you and they are partners in shared inquiry, and that you will be asking questions you care about and need their ideas to resolve. Encourage students to raise questions of their own and to speak to each other rather than always to you.

In addition to explaining how Shared Inquiry Discussion works, it is vital that your students understand the guidelines the class will follow during discussion and the reasons for them. For this purpose, we recommend distributing the handout on the next page before your first discussion.

Discussion Guidelines

Come to discussion with your book, a pen or pencil, a notebook, and an open mind. In Shared Inquiry Discussion, everyone, including the leader, considers a question with more than one reasonable answer and weighs the evidence for different answers. The goal of discussion is for each of you to develop an answer that satisfies you personally.

Following the rules outlined below will make for a better discussion:

★ **Read the selection before participating in the discussion.** This ensures that all participants are equally prepared to talk about the ideas in the work and helps prevent talk that would distract the group from its purpose.

★ **Support your ideas with evidence from the text.** This keeps the discussion focused on understanding the selection. It will enable the group to weigh textual support for different answers and to choose intelligently among them.

★ **Discuss the ideas in the selection, and try to understand them fully before exploring issues that go beyond the selection.** Weighing evidence for different interpretations is essential before exploring related issues or deciding whether we agree with the author.

★ **Listen to others and respond to them directly.** Shared inquiry is about the give-and-take of ideas, a willingness to listen to others and to talk to them respectfully. Directing your comments and questions to other group members, not always to the leader, will make the discussion livelier and more dynamic.

★ **Expect the leader to ask questions, rather than answer them.** The leader's role is to keep discussion effective and interesting by listening and asking questions. The leader's goal is to help participants develop their own ideas, with everyone (the leader included) gaining a new understanding in the process.

Building Your Answer Activity Page

We recommend that before each discussion you distribute copies of the Building Your Answer page (see pp. 22–23) to students. Ask them to take about five minutes to write down their initial thoughts about your opening question before discussion begins. Doing so encourages students to think more deeply about their answers and allows quieter students to frame a response that they will feel confident sharing. After discussion, students can finish their Building Your Answer pages in class or as homework.

Leading Discussion Effectively

Leading Shared Inquiry Discussion is a process that you can expect to become easier over time. If you lead discussion regularly, both you and your class will grow more confident and comfortable with it. The following suggestions should help you.

Begin the discussion with a real question. Ask a question that you are genuinely struggling to answer yourself—not a test question, a leading question, or a teaching question. Can you answer your own question in at least two different ways that are supported by the text?

Share your curiosity and enthusiasm. Lead with your curiosity, not your knowledge. By sharing what you are curious about and admitting what you don't know, you model the attitude you are asking students to adopt.

Encourage students to think for themselves. Try to remain in the role of leader by only asking questions. You should not answer questions or endorse ideas by making statements such as "Good idea" or, especially, "I agree" or "I disagree."

Listen carefully and ask follow-up questions often. Careful, attentive listening is the most important skill a shared inquiry leader can cultivate. Follow-up questions—spontaneous questions that arise from a leader's ability to listen closely and respond directly to students— drive and sustain an effective discussion. They help students develop their ideas and help everyone think more carefully about the relationships between different answers.

The best follow-up questions can be as simple as *Can you repeat that?* or *What made you think so?* Follow-up questions can

- **Clarify comments.** *What do you mean by that? Can you explain that another way?*

- **Get evidence.** *What in the poem gave you that idea? What did the character say or do that made you think so?*

- **Test and develop ideas.** *If you think that's what the character means, then why does this happen in the story? Is there anything in the story that doesn't seem to go with your answer?*

- **Elicit additional opinions.** *What do you think about what she just said? Do you agree with that idea? Does anyone have an idea we haven't heard yet?*

Track student participation with a seating chart. Keep track of discussion by marking which students participate and how. A check mark by a student's name can indicate that a student offered an answer, the notation "NA" can indicate that a student had no answer when asked to speak, and so on. The chart can help you identify patterns of participation in your class and evaluate students' contributions.

Ask students to look back at the text frequently. Asking students to find passages that support their answers helps everyone think about the specifics of the selection and keeps discussion on track. Revisiting the text and asking students to read portions aloud helps clear up misunderstandings and prompts new questions and interpretations. You might even go into discussion with a couple of passages in mind that you think are relevant to exploring your opening question.

Return often to the opening question. To keep discussion focused, ask students how their thoughts relate to the question you posed at the beginning of the discussion. This reminds everyone of the problem the group is trying to solve and helps students consider it in depth.

Create opportunities for quieter students to speak. It's easy for talkative students to dominate discussion, with quieter ones getting shut out. Marking participation on a seating chart can alert you to this pattern; if it happens in your group, try asking quieter students if they've heard an answer they agree with or what answer they wrote down on the Building Your Answer page.

Encourage students to speak directly to one another. If you address students by name and ask them to explain their ideas to one another, you will foster an environment of open inquiry and respect.

End discussion when your group has discussed the opening question in depth. You will usually be able to sense when your group has considered a number of answers to the opening question and most students could, if asked, provide their own "best answer" to the question. You may wish to check by asking *Are there any different ideas we haven't heard yet? Is there any part of the text we should look at before wrapping up?* Remind students that they will not reach consensus on an answer, because the selections support multiple interpretations. Having students complete the Building Your Answer page is an effective way to help them consider how discussion has changed or expanded their initial answers. If students seem eager to talk about ideas in the selection that relate to their own lives, you can use one of the Writing After Discussion prompts for discussion as a class or in small groups, as well as for writing.

Periodically ask students to assess their work in discussion. After every two or three discussions, ask students to share their thoughts on how discussion is going and how it might be improved. Help the class set specific goals for improvement in areas such as supporting their opinions with evidence from the text, staying focused on the meaning of the text under discussion, and speaking directly to other students rather than just to the leader.

Building Your Answer in
Shared Inquiry Discussion

Name: _____

Selection: _____

Your leader's opening question: _____

_____

_____

_____

Your answer before discussion: _____

_____

_____

_____

How did discussion affect your answer? Did it change your mind? Provide additional support for your answer?

Make you aware of additional issues? _____

_____

_____

_____

_____

Your answer after discussion: _____

_____

_____

_____

What in the selection helped you decide on this answer? _____

_____

Writing After Discussion

- Gives students practice in systematically articulating, supporting, and developing their ideas

- Stimulates original thought and prompts students to connect what they read to their own experiences and opinions

- Helps students build a commitment to reading and critical thinking by continuing their thoughtful engagement with a selection's ideas

Because Shared Inquiry Discussion requires students to consider questions of meaning in depth, it is an excellent springboard to further exploring ideas through writing. Having students write an interpretive essay explaining and supporting the answer they developed on the Building Your Answer page is always an option for writing after discussion.

In addition, the Writing After Discussion prompts included in each unit give students opportunities to use different types of writing to connect the issues in a selection with their own experiences or to further explore the ideas raised by a selection. Although suggested as optional homework assignments, some of these topics can provide the basis for further classroom discussion.

Vocabulary

The Perfection Learning student anthologies provide some short definitions of unfamiliar words as footnotes and a concept vocabulary at the beginning of the book. There are a number of other ways you can help students expand their vocabularies and learn strategies for understanding words that are new to them:

- Encourage students to raise questions about words they find unusual or confusing during the Sharing Questions session.

- Ask questions that guide students to search the context for clues to a word's meaning.

- Have students keep lists of new words that they find interesting, unusual, or helpful.

Assessment

Whether or not you assign a grade for participation in Great Books, sharing your goals with students gives them a clear idea of what they are working toward, or what is expected of them, and helps them perform better. Evaluating students' progress and your own performance can also help you become a better leader, since there is a direct connection between what you do and the quality of discussion. Your choice of follow-up questions and willingness to listen will encourage students to develop their own ideas, support them with evidence from the text, and work together to explore the selection as a group. Progress as well as performance in reading, oral language, writing, and thinking skills should all be considered when you evaluate your students.

For the evaluation of oral work, your seating charts will provide a record of students' participation and the ideas they expressed in Shared Inquiry Discussion. Comparing these notes from week to week will help you give students feedback on their progress, individually or as a group.

A portfolio can show each student's improvements and strengths. When you collect students' written work, including the Building Your Answer page as well as any Writing After Discussion assignments, you might ask them for all of the work on one unit of their choice or from units covered both earlier and later in the semester. Let students select and evaluate some of their own pieces.

Students' ability to express themselves in writing is not always the same as their ability to express themselves in discussion. To promote critical thinking, focus on the content of what a student has written, rather than the mechanics. You can always have students work on mechanics during a revision stage.

Writing and assessment are covered in specialized consultation days offered as advanced professional development for leaders of Shared Inquiry Discussion. Call the Great Books Foundation at 1-800-222-5870 or visit www.greatbooks.org for more information about all of our professional development offerings and anthologies of literature.

DISCUSSION UNIT 1

Prospective Immigrants Please Note

ADRIENNE RICH

NOTE: Although this is the first piece in the book, you might want to return to it at the end of your work on *From There to Here,* when students' responses to the poem and to the Writing After Discussion questions will be informed by the variety of immigrant experiences they have read about.

Text Opener

Imagine that students from another country who are planning to immigrate to the United States have contacted you. You expect them to be excited, and they do, in fact, have high expectations, but they are also apprehensive. Why might they be apprehensive and what advice would you give to guide them?

Directed Notes

Mark the **negative** consequences of going through or not going through the door with **N,** and the **positive** consequences with **P.**

Interpretive Questions for Discussion

Is the speaker trying to persuade prospective immigrants to go through the door?

1. What is the door that the speaker refers to?

2. Why does the speaker say that "remembering your name" is a "risk" for an immigrant?

3. Why do "things look at you doubly" when you go through the door? What are the "things"? Why must you "look back / and let them happen"?

4. Why does the speaker say that "much will blind you," if you do not go through the door?

5. Why does the speaker say that it is "only" a door?

6. Does the speaker believe that people have a choice about whether or not to go through the door?

Writing After Discussion

1. Do you believe that people have a choice about whether or not to go through the door?

2. What makes some people take risks in situations where others play it safe?

3. Write a fictional dialogue in which one person tries to convince another either to go through "the door" or not.

4. If you are an immigrant yourself, you may want to respond to the poet directly. What would you say? Express your thoughts and feelings in a poem.

DISCUSSION UNIT 2

The Hardships of a Greenhorn

MICHAEL PUPIN

Text Opener

Write down five things a new immigrant to the United States should do to fit in and become successful. Prioritize them from 1 to 5.

Directed Notes

Mark places where Michael thinks, speaks, or behaves in a way that will help him overcome his "greenhorn" status with ☆.

Interpretive Questions for Discussion

Why is Michael "disturbed" when the Vila's mother comments that "the sooner you drop your Serbian notions the sooner you will become an American"?

1. When he first starts out, why does Michael compare himself to "a strong man ready to run a race"?

2. When Michael discovers that the prune pie is filled with pits and he has been cheated, why doesn't he get angry? Why does he tell himself that he has to serve an "apprenticeship as a greenhorn" before he can establish a "claim to any recognition"?

3. Why does Michael believe that something must be wrong with his judgment when he decides that Serb peasants are superior to American peasants?

4. When he first meets the young girl, why is Michael so "certain that if there ever was a Vila this young girl was one"? Why does he continue to think of her as "my American Vila"?

5. Why is Michael's "highest ambition" to show himself worthy of the title "smart"?

6. Why does Michael find it "strange" that the Vila's mother assumes that he wants to become an American?

7. What does Michael think it means to "become an American"?

8. What is Michael's goal in coming to America?

Writing After Discussion

1. What does it mean to "become an American"? Can a person do this without becoming a U.S. citizen?

2. Do you agree with Michael that "nothing counts so much in the immigrant's bid for promotion to a grade above that of a greenhorn as the knowledge of the English language"?

3. What do the Vila and her mother think of Michael? Write a fictional dialogue in which these two characters discuss their feelings and opinions about Michael.

4. How should someone go about the challenging task of learning English? Using the events of the story and your own experiences, create a pamphlet called "English for Greenhorns" in which you provide and explain five pieces of advice that you would give to someone who wants to learn English.

DISCUSSION UNIT 3

Bananas

MICHAEL GOLD

Text Opener

If you had to do something humiliating or demeaning in order to survive, how would you cope?

Directed Notes

Mark places where you think that a character's reaction is **reasonable** with **R,** and places where you think that a character's reaction is **unreasonable** with **U.**

Interpretive Questions for Discussion

Why does the author find it hard to be optimistic when his father says that he will have luck in America?

1. Why does the author say that he was poisoned with a "morbid proletarian sense of responsibility"? What or whom does he feel responsible for?

2. Why is the author "frantic" and almost unable to quit yelling when his father tells him to stop?

3. Why does the author's father call himself a greenhorn but think of his son as an American?

4. Why does the author's father ask his son to promise him that he will be rich when he grows up?

5. Why does the author promise that he will be rich when he grows up?

6. Why does the author's father believe that luck will come to his son as an American?

7. Why does the author describe his father's optimism at the end of the story as "naïve"?

8. Why is the author so despondent at the end of the story?

Writing After Discussion

1. Do you agree that an immigrant's success or failure is due mainly to luck?

2. Imagine that you are an immigrant to the United States. Would you feel encouraged or intimidated by knowing that your parents counted on you to succeed?

3. You may have heard the saying, "Money doesn't buy happiness." Compose several interview questions that explore people's opinions about the relationship between jobs, money, and happiness. Interview three people representing different generations. State your findings in a report.

DISCUSSION UNIT 4

Tears of Autumn

YOSHIKO UCHIDA

Text Opener

What personal qualities must a person have in order to leave his or her homeland and journey to a new country? Choose five qualities and be prepared to explain your reasons for selecting them.

Directed Notes

Mark places where Hana seems to **conform** to the culture around her with **C**, and places where she seems to be **breaking away** with **B**.

Interpretive Questions for Discussion

What is the "small hope trembling inside" of Hana as she sets sail for the United States?

1. Why does Hana suddenly become aware that she wants "to escape the smothering strictures of life in her village"?

2. Why is it important to Hana "to find the real man" in Taro's letters? Why does Hana keep thinking of Taro as "this lonely man"?

3. Why does the author tell us that Hana has "five more years of schooling than her older sister"?

4. When Hana meets Taro at the pier, is she pleased or disappointed with the man she will marry?

5. Are we to believe that Hana is conforming to or breaking away from the traditions of her culture by traveling to America to become Taro's wife?

6. Why is the title of the story "Tears of Autumn," when the story ends in laughter?

Writing After Discussion

1. After immigrating, why do some people distance themselves as much as possible from their native culture, while others strive to maintain it?

2. Is it possible or desirable for people to leave their native cultures completely behind when they immigrate to another country?

3. Should Hana have left her family to join Taro Takeda in the United States, or should she have stayed in Japan? Write a letter to Hana in which you explain why you think her decision was either admirable or foolish.

4. What do you think Taro Takeda felt as he waited for Hana's arrival? Write a poem in which you take his perspective and express your hopes and fears.

Discussion Unit 5

The New Colossus

EMMA LAZARUS

Your Tired, Your Poor, Your Undocumented Foreigners

CHARLES OSGOOD

Text Opener

Read Emma Lazarus's poem "The New Colossus" on page 15. Write a brief answer to one or both of the following questions:

1. What groups of people might believe that the "Mother of Exiles" lifts her lamp especially for them?

2. Is the Statue of Liberty a good symbol for the United States?

Directed Notes

Mark places where Osgood seems to be **supportive** of U.S. immigration policy with +, and places where he seems to be **critical** of U.S. policy with –.

Interpretive Questions for Discussion

Is Osgood criticizing would-be immigrants or the United States and its immigration policy?

1. Why does Osgood say that, although the reasons given for immigrating to the United States "are usually political, . . . one suspects that economic . . . circumstances may be at the heart of it"?

2. Why does Osgood turn Emma Lazarus's words into a numbered list showing "six kinds of people who want to move to the United States"?

3. Does Osgood think it's right that "if you are rich you probably stand a better chance of being let in"?

4. Does Osgood believe that there are valid reasons for entering the United States?

5. Does Osgood want us to think that the United States should be able to "absorb the homeless from elsewhere in the world"?

6. Why does Osgood tell us about the young professional who "knew about the Iron Curtain but had never heard of the Golden Door"?

NOTE: Before discussing the following questions, students should read "Looking North" by Roberto Suro (pp. 128–131) and "Huddled Masses" by Michael Satchell (pp. 133–134).

Would Osgood say that the Cubans in "Looking North" and the Kosovars in "Huddled Masses" deserve the same or different treatment by the United States?

1. Satchell calls the fleeing of Kosovo's ethnic Albanians "Europe's greatest forced migration . . . since World War II," and Suro says of the Cubans that "politics forced them to go. Their pocketbooks drove them." How would Osgood perceive these situations?

2. Would Osgood agree with the Cubans who are determined that "the Americans will not keep us away," despite the "laws and barbed wire" of the United States?

3. Why does Suro consistently refer to the people he writes about as "travelers" on a "journey," instead of as "refugees" or "victims" as Satchell does?

4. Why does Suro say that a "dream of bright lights draws people north," but end by saying that "beyond them, there was nothing but darkness and the sound of waves"? What would Osgood think of the "dream of bright lights"?

Writing After Discussion

1. Should people in desperate situations remain undeterred by the "laws and barbed wire" that might keep them out of the United States?

2. Are Emma Lazarus's words too idealistic?

3. What aspects of the current U.S. immigration situation seem ironic or absurd to you? Express your own opinion on the immigration issue in the form of a political cartoon.

Titles of Related Interest from the Great Books Foundation

The Great Books Foundation publishes the following readings on related topics, along with interpretive questions for discussion, note-taking suggestions, and writing activities. The Junior Great Books series, *A Latino National Conversation: Reading on Assimilation, Modern American Poetry,* and *The Will of the People: Readings in American Democracy* are available for purchase on our Web site or by calling 1-800-222-5870.

From Junior Great Books Series 6, Second Semester

The White Umbrella • GISH JEN

Surprised and a little embarrassed when her mother gets a job and is late picking her up from her piano lesson, the twelve-year-old Chinese American narrator feels divided loyalties when her piano teacher, Miss Crosman, is kind to her.

From Junior Great Books Series 8

Rules of the Game (from *The Joy Luck Club*) • AMY TAN

The narrator of "Rules of the Game" is nine-year-old chess champion Waverly Jong. Finding her way between her Chinese mother's ambitions for her and the American culture into which her family is assimilating, Waverly seeks her own "invisible strength" and a way to be her own person.

A Latino National Conversation: Readings on Assimilation

This anthology, which includes selections by Julia Alvarez, Judith Ortiz Cofer, Oscar Hijuelos, and Richard Rodriguez, focuses on the efforts of various Latino writers to preserve their ethnic and cultural heritage while adapting to life in the United States.

Modern American Poetry

The many voices in this anthology, which begins with Walt Whitman, express the range and vigor of modern American poetry. Among them, Gary Soto takes up issues of the urban barrio, the migrant worker, and the tenant farmer, searching the present and the past for their Chicano identity and spiritual origins. Rita Dove, Martín Espada, Donald Hall, Linda Hogan, Yusef Komunyakaa, Li-Young Lee, and Naomi Shihab Nye lend other perspectives to the American experience.

The Will of the People: Readings in American Democracy

The United States is a nation of immigrants. Reexamine core texts from the history of American democracy, including the Declaration of Independence, the Emancipation Proclamation, Abraham Lincoln's second inaugural address, Sojourner Truth's address to the first annual meeting of the American Equal Rights Association, and "Let America Be America Again," by Langston Hughes.